Cause, Effect and Chaos!

In the Human Body

Author Paul Mason
with artwork by Mark Ruffle

WAYLAND

First published in Great Britain in 2018
by Wayland
Copyright © Hodder and Stoughton, 2018

Series editor: Paul Rockett
Series design and illustration: Mark Ruffle
www.rufflebrothers.com

HB ISBN 978 1 5263 0574 9
PB ISBN 978 1 5263 0575 6

Printed in China

Wayland, an imprint of
Hachette Children's Group
Part of Hodder and Stoughton
Carmelite House
50 Victoria Embankment
London EC4Y 0DZ

An Hachette UK Company
www.hachette.co.uk

Contents

Cause and Effect

What causes events to happen? Usually they are the effect of something that happened just before.

You can probably think of a few examples from your own life:

You listen to your swimming teacher, instead of putting your head underwater when she's speaking.

You finally work out how to swim excellent front crawl. Now you might become Olympic champion!

Of course, not every action has a good effect:

You ignore the hissing sound coming from the front wheel of your bike.

Hisssss

Next day you have a flat tyre. Riding your bike proves harder and you go more slowly.

Chaos! You are late for your swimming lesson and do not become Olympic champion after all.

Inside your body, cause and effect usually help you stay healthy.

You feel tired and without energy.

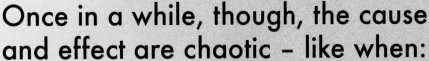

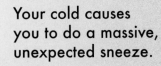

you go to sleep.

Next day you wake up feeling alert and full of energy again.

Once in a while, though, the cause and effect are chaotic – like when:

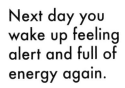

Your cold causes you to do a massive, unexpected sneeze.

You have to spend ages cleaning snot off your game controller.

Achoo!

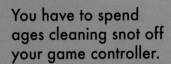

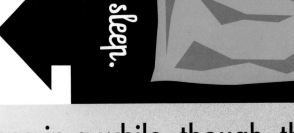

5

Most of the time, you don't notice your body working. Your heart and lungs, for example, usually just get on with their jobs.

Once in a while, though, your body comes under extra strain – like when you're late for the cinema ...

Run faster!
You're late!

A message is sent from your brain to your legs:

Run!

Brain

Heart

Your heart beats faster, so that your blood can carry energy to your muscles as quickly as possible.

Your legs start working harder than usual, which quickly uses up the energy in your muscles.

Your leg muscles need more energy! A message is sent upstairs: urgent, energy required!

Muscles

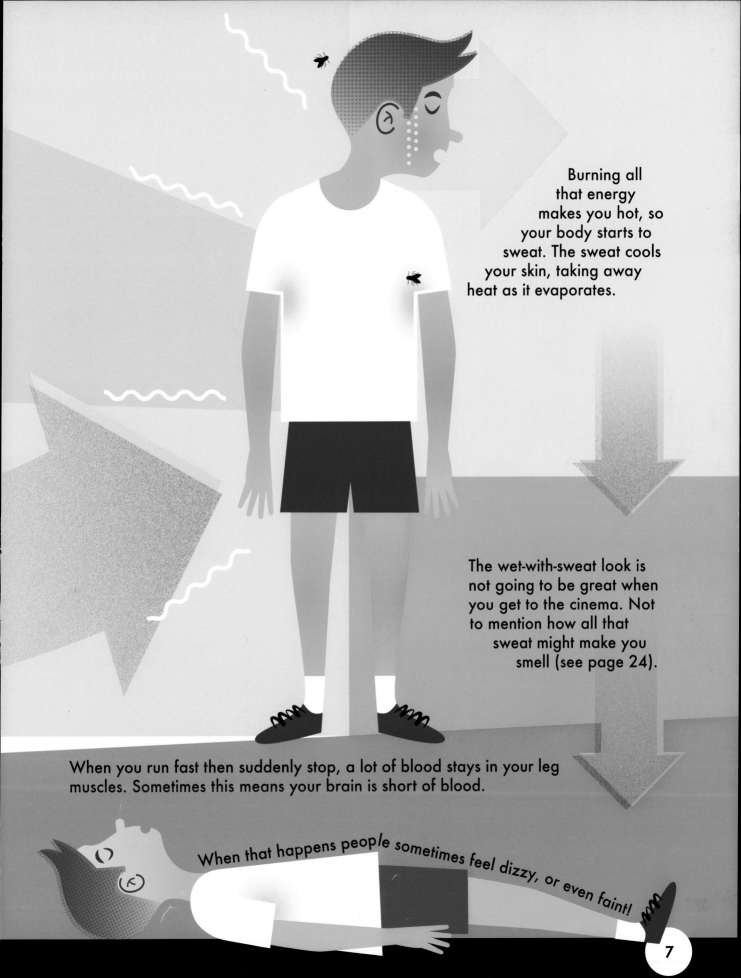

Burning all that energy makes you hot, so your body starts to sweat. The sweat cools your skin, taking away heat as it evaporates.

The wet-with-sweat look is not going to be great when you get to the cinema. Not to mention how all that sweat might make you smell (see page 24).

When you run fast then suddenly stop, a lot of blood stays in your leg muscles. Sometimes this means your brain is short of blood.

When that happens people sometimes feel dizzy, or even faint!

Breaking Bones

Your bones are incredibly strong, and withstand everyday knocks and bumps. However, if a force is too great they can break.

An adult human skeleton is made up of 206 bones. Bones provide support for our bodies and help form our shape.

Bones break when too much pressure or stress is placed on them. A break or a crack in a bone is called a fracture.

Most bone fractures are caused by falls and accidents.

Fracture

When you have broken a bone, you may feel a pain in the surrounding area and feel dizzy and faint.

Simple fractures are broken bones that do not poke through the skin.

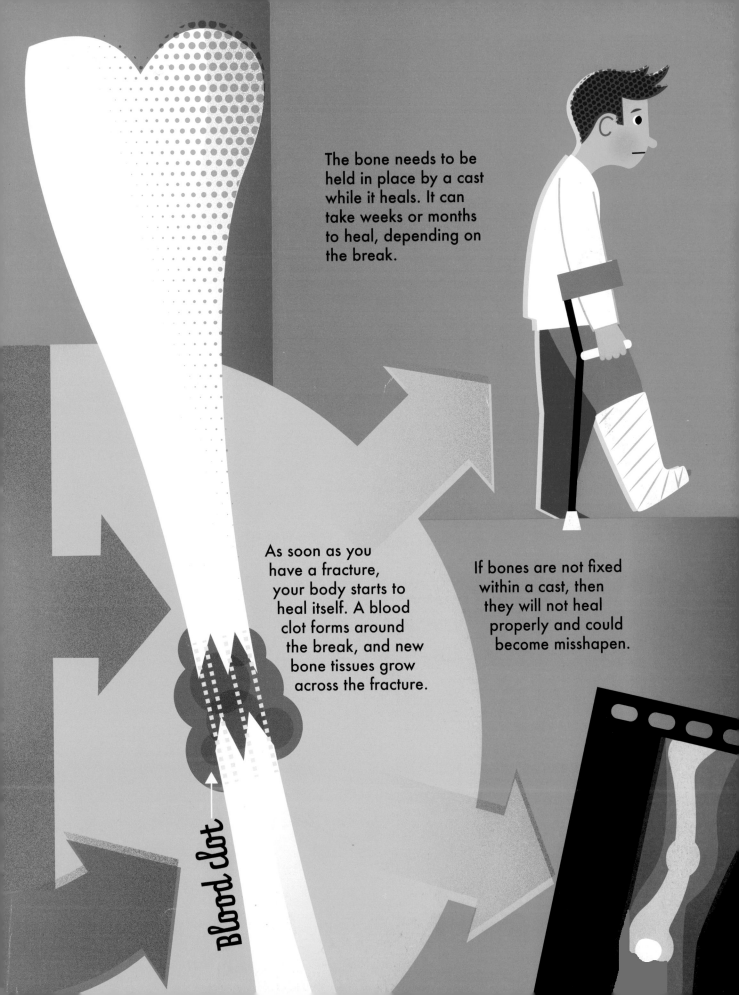

The bone needs to be held in place by a cast while it heals. It can take weeks or months to heal, depending on the break.

As soon as you have a fracture, your body starts to heal itself. A blood clot forms around the break, and new bone tissues grow across the fracture.

If bones are not fixed within a cast, then they will not heal properly and could become misshapen.

Blood clot

Fuelling Up

Your body gets its fuel from food and drink. But how, exactly, does your body start turning pizza into power, eggs into energy, burgers into bounce?

The process begins before you even bite into food, when your mouth starts 'watering', producing extra **saliva.**

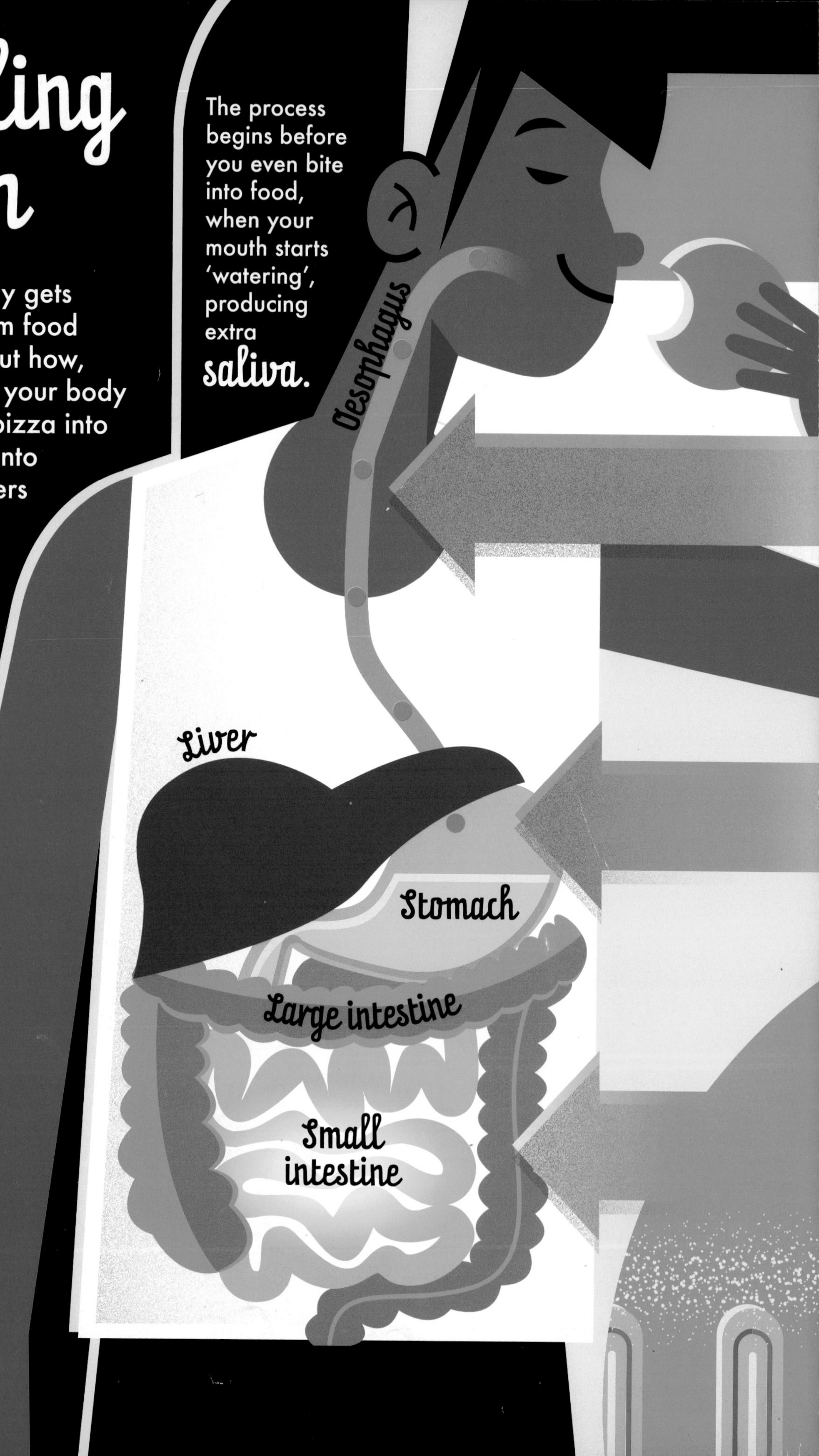

Oesophagus

Liver

Stomach

Large intestine

Small intestine

You bite off a piece of food and chew. Your teeth mash the food into smaller bits, which mix with saliva and become **food sludge**.

If your stomach senses you've swallowed something that's going to make you ill, it gives a massive, muscly squeeze. All the food sludge is vomited back the way it came.

The sludge gets swallowed and travels down your oesophagus to your stomach.

Swallowing happens using muscle power, not gravity. That's why you can drink water standing on your head.

Chaos!

The sludge is churned about in stomach acid and enzymes. The acid is strong enough for a single drop to eat through a wooden table! The acid turns the sludge into liquid.

You are protected from your stomach acid by a special stomach lining that's constantly replacing itself.

A valve in your stomach opens, and the liquid food moves into your intestines.

In your intestines, the nutrients from your food are removed and absorbed into your blood. They are carried away in your blood, for use elsewhere in your body.

Most absorption happens in the small intestine, via tiny projecting fingers called villi. Inside these are blood vessels.

<--- *villi*

Blurgh!

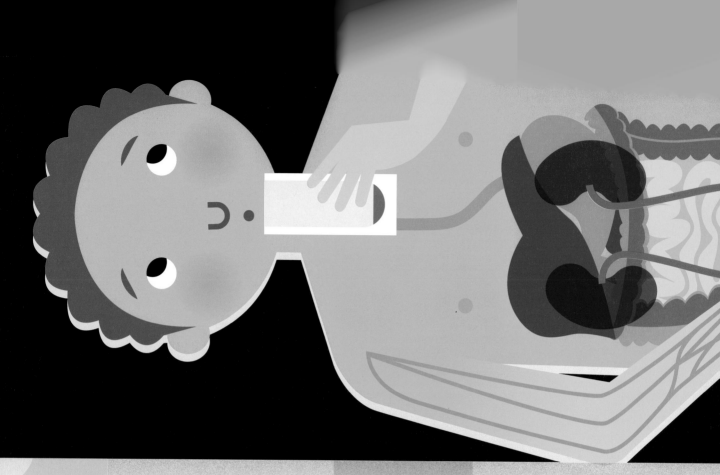

Waste into Wee

Your body needs liquid to survive. In fact, you can live about seven times longer without food than water.*

The liquid in your body does all kinds of jobs. One of them is helping to flush out waste products.

*Experts say that most people can live three weeks without food, but only three days without water.

You swallow water just like food (see page 11). It travels down your oesophagus, into your stomach and then into your intestines.

Oesophagus

Stomach

In your intestines, most of the water is absorbed into your blood. In fact, over 95 per cent of the water you take in is absorbed here.

Intestines

Blood is nearly

80

per cent water.

Usually it's easy to wait until you reach a toilet.

Don't wait too long, though. If too much pressure builds up in your bladder, it just HAS to empty itself.

Disaster!

Your heart pumps blood around your body, transporting nutrients, oxygen and other important chemicals. Blood also collects waste products.

The blood reaches your kidneys, where it is cleaned. Waste products are removed, along with some of the water.

The waste liquid, called urine, travels from your kidneys to your bladder. Once your bladder is full, it sends a message to your brain:

'Time to wee!'

Blood

kidneys

Bladder

Allergic Reactions

Some people are allergic to things they touch, breathe in or eat.

Common allergies include nuts, pollen, milk, pet hair, dust and exhaust fumes from cars.

milk

A few people are allergic to insect stings or bites. No one is allergic to homework.

Attack!

Your nervous system signals your body to release special defence chemicals. The chemicals rush to attack the allergen.

When your body comes into contact with an allergen – something it doesn't think should be there – an allergic reaction begins.

While attacking the allergen, the chemicals may also give you itchy, watery eyes, make you sneeze or cause a red rash on your skin.

Sick

If you have eaten an allergen, your body usually vomits it right back up (see page 11 for more about this).

In some people's bodies, allergens cause

total chaos.

Their blood stops circulating properly. Their mouth, tongue and throat start to swell, making it hard to breathe.

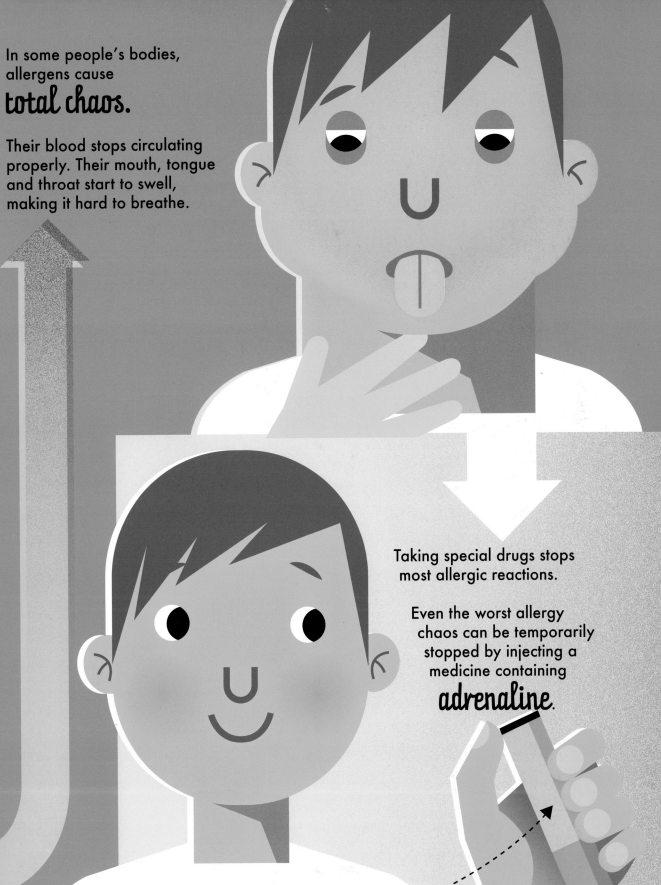

Taking special drugs stops most allergic reactions.

Even the worst allergy chaos can be temporarily stopped by injecting a medicine containing **adrenaline**.

EpiPens are used to inject adrenaline into the body if someone has a serious allergic reaction. It gives them time to get to the hospital for further treatment, if it is needed.

lusic, Maestro!

What actually happens inside your body when you put in the earbuds and ess play?

nd reaches your ears in the n of vibrations in the air.

The vibrations travel down your outer ear to your eardrum, a thin skin that stretches across your ear hole.

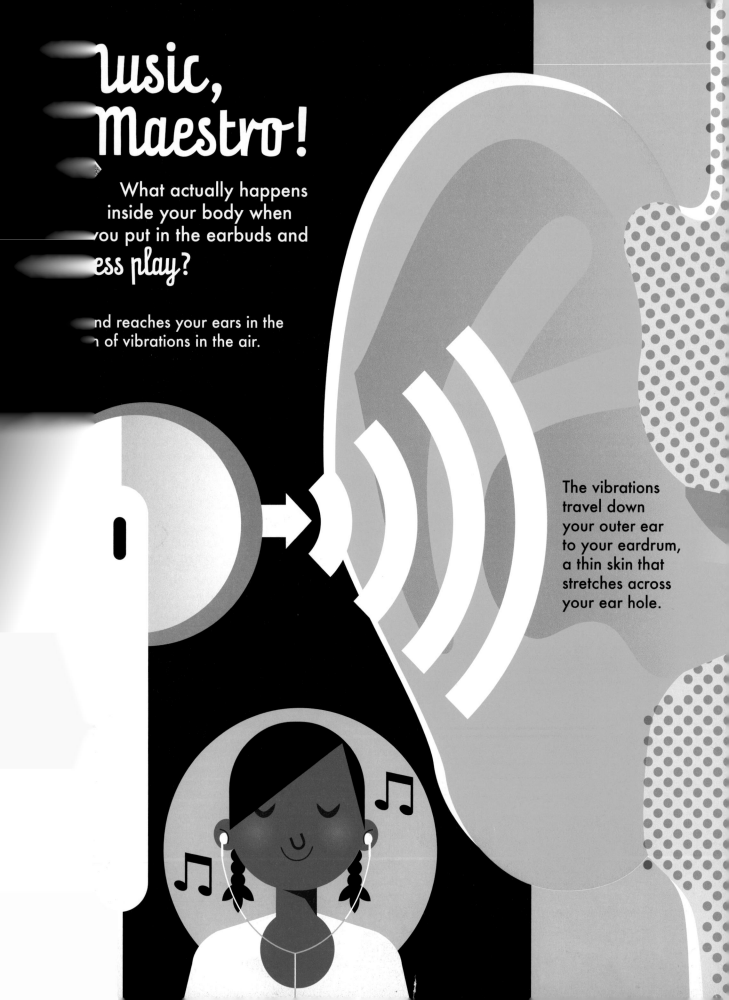

The vibrations make your eardrum wobble, which passes them on to three tiny bones inside your middle ear.

These bones – the smallest in your body – act as a chain. They pass the vibrations along to your inner ear.

Your inner ear contains tiny hair cells. Their tips are moved by the vibrations. The hair cells turn each movement into a tiny electrical signal to your brain.

Hair cells

Different hair cells are moved by different sounds. The exact combination of cells that move tells your brain what you are hearing.

Eardrum

Bones

Inner ear

Loud noises cause the tips of the hair cells to bend, or even break. The whole cell dies, and your hearing is just a tiny bit worse.

If this happens too often, **you start to go deaf.**

Catching a Cold

You can't catch a cold by going outside with wet hair and no hat, whatever grown-ups tell you. So how DO you get one?

Colds are caused by miniature creatures called viruses. They arrive in droplets of fluid from someone who has a cold.

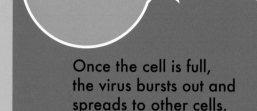

Once the cell is full, the virus bursts out and spreads to other cells.

When someone with a cold coughs or sneezes, the virus-carrying droplets spray out.

Achoo!

It burrows inside a cell in your nose or throat and starts reproducing itself.

If you breathe in droplets or touch something with them on it, the virus spreads to you.

The spreading virus gives you a sore throat.
You start coughing and sneezing, which spreads the virus to other people.

Your body
sends special
**white blood
cells**
to fight the virus.

Some of the white blood cells kill the invading virus cells.

Others stick to the *virus* so it cannot reproduce.

It usually takes *a few days* for your body to defeat the cold virus.

After the virus is defeated, your white blood cells remember it. They will fight it off more quickly next time.

Shocked into Action

Everyone gets a sudden shock sometimes. Like, someone steps in front of your speeding skateboard, you spot a bear in the bushes, or you're asked to do the washing-up.

Your whole body gets ready for action REALLY quickly, without you thinking about it.

Hypothalamus

A part of your brain called the hypothalamus tells your body to release a chemical called adrenaline.

Heart

Your heart beats faster and you breathe more quickly, sending extra oxygen to your muscles.

This whole reaction supercharges your body, ready to either fight off danger or run away from it.

Pupils

The pupils of your eyes get bigger, making it easier for you to focus on hazards.

Muscles

Your muscles tense up – even the tiny ones that move the hairs on your arms and the back of your neck, which stand up on end.

Fight or flight mode has one unfortunate side effect. Without warning, your body may get rid of waste products (i.e. urine and faeces).

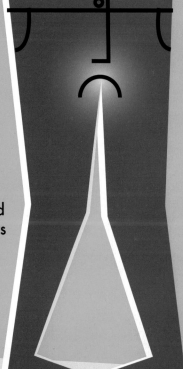

Yikes!

A Load of (Tooth) Rot

Your teeth are brilliantly designed for eating, but they do have one big problem. They share your mouth with millions of bacteria.

These bacteria mean your teeth are constantly teetering on the brink of a rotten future. Only battling the bacteria can save them!

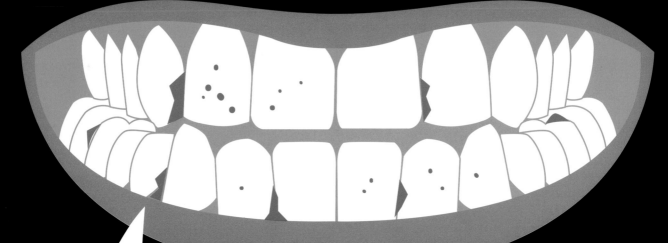

When you eat something, tiny pieces of food are left behind in your mouth. Many of the pieces collect on your teeth.

Stinky

The bacteria in your mouth start eating the tiny bits of food. They especially like fizzy drinks, cakes and chocolate.

As they eat, the bacteria let off a stinky gas – which you breathe all over people. *Yeuw!*

The acid makes little holes called cavities in your tooth's hard outer layer, the enamel.

The bacteria also release acid.

Now the acid can eat away at the soft inner parts of the tooth, which *really hurts*.

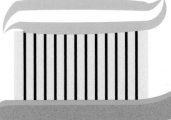

Fortunately, to battle the bacteria all you have to do is brush them off with a toothbrush and toothpaste.

The bacteria are always lurking, though, so this is a never-ending fight.

The holes need to be filled – otherwise the whole tooth might one day have to be taken out.

Ouch!

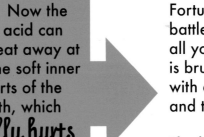

It's the Pits

Humans stink! At least, they do unless they stop the smell their skin naturally creates.

But just what is it that actually makes people smelly?

As the **sweat is released**, bacteria living on your skin start to eat it.

There are hundreds of different bacteria on your skin.

Stink!

When you get hot and bothered, you sweat. Some of the sweat is a special kind called apocrine sweat. Your armpits produce a lot of apocrine sweat.

Apocrine sweat is your armpit bacteria's absolute favourite meal!

As they eat sweat, the bacteria produce acid and release gas. These sometimes smell cheesy, sometimes vinegary.

They never smell good, though.

Soap

To get rid of the smell, you have to wash off the bacteria and the sweat they eat.

If you cannot wash, the smell stays with you. In fact, the thought of being smelly might make you hot and bothered all over again. As a result you sweat more ...

... the bacteria have more to eat ...

... and you smell even worse!

Getting Hiccups

Hiccups are a mystery. We know what they are, but we don't really know why they happen.

Hiccups begin when a thin layer of muscle called your diaphragm, which helps you breathe, goes wrong. It tightens up with a sudden jerk.

Trachea

Right lung

Left lung

Trachea

Diaphragm

The jerk yanks down on the base of your lungs. They suddenly get bigger.

Your expanding lungs suck air into your mouth, really fast.

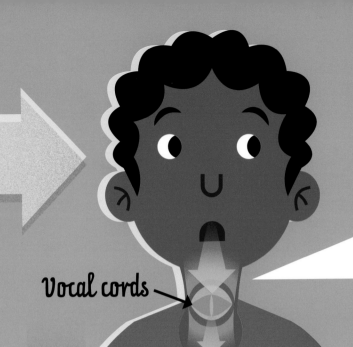

The rush of air hits your vocal cords, which close up to protect themselves. This stops the air getting to your lungs, and makes you go ...

Hic!

Vocal cords

If you want to make your hiccups stop, you have to wait: there is no cure. That hasn't stopped people trying to find cures, including:

Drinking a glass of water standing on your head.

Getting a sudden *fright*.

Eating a big spoonful of peanut butter.

Drinking water through a paper towel.

None of these work.

Usually, hiccups just go away on their own after a few minutes – but the world record for having hiccups is 68 years.*

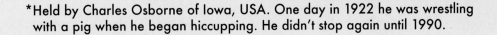

*Held by Charles Osborne of Iowa, USA. One day in 1922 he was wrestling with a pig when he began hiccupping. He didn't stop again until 1990.

Growing Up and Growing Old

The longest chain of cause and effect in the human body is one nobody can avoid. It is being born, growing up and getting old.

The chain starts when a sperm cell from your father joins an egg cell from your mother.

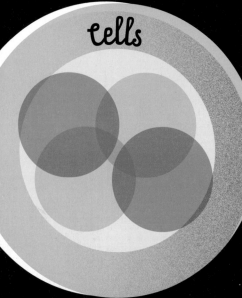

Cells

After about 40 weeks, the baby is born. It still has a lot of growing to do.

By the time they are two, most youngsters can talk and walk. They keep growing and learning new skills.

The new cell divides, again and again, making bone cells, heart cells, brain cells and other kinds.

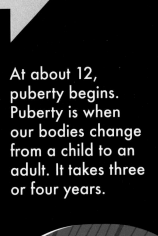

At about 12, puberty begins. Puberty is when our bodies change from a child to an adult. It takes three or four years.

12

After puberty, human bodies keep developing. At about 30 they reach their physical peak.

By the time they are 60, humans are usually less flexible, with weaker bones and muscles.

In old age, people's bodies work less and less well.

Eventually, they die. Most people live to about **80** years old – though some are still alive at over 100.

People find it harder to remember things.

Glossary

adrenaline a chemical (or hormone) produced by the body in response to anger, fright or excitement. It is also the active medicine in an EpiPen. It makes the heart beat faster and causes muscles in the lungs to relax

allergen substance that causes an allergic reaction, in which the body tries to fight off the allergen (even though the allergen is otherwise harmless)

allergic responding badly to a substance, for example pollen, peanuts or insect stings

cell tiny building blocks that make up your body. In total you contain billions of cells

clot blob of liquid that has become thicker and started to harden

diaphragm thin dome of muscle attached to the bottom of your lungs. When the muscle tightens it pulls down on the lungs, making them bigger, which draws air in

droplet small drop, like in the spray that comes out of a huffer bottle

evaporate change from liquid into vapour

faeces solid waste from the human body, also known as poo

faint suddenly become unconscious

inject give someone a drug using a hollow needle to put it in their body

misshapen not in its normal or natural shape

nutrient substance that our bodies can use to grow, stay alive or repair damage

oesophagus tube leading from your throat to your stomach, sometimes called the 'food pipe'

physical peak time when your body works as well as it ever will

pollen tiny, usually microscopic grains that are released by flowers as part of plant reproduction

saliva watery liquid released in your mouth as part of the digestive process

tissue body tissues are groups of cells of a similar type, such as skin or bone or heart tissue

trachea sometimes called the 'windpipe', this is the tube leading from your mouth to your lungs

vibrate make small, fast movements back and forth without stopping

Finding Out More

Body places

The Science Museum
Exhibition Road
South Kensington
London SW7 2DD

The museum often has special exhibitions about the human body and how it works. It also has a good website with loads of fascinating facts about how your body works.

The Science Museum website is at sciencemuseum.org.uk. To get to the human body section, go to sciencemuseum.org.uk/whoami/findoutmore/yourbody.aspx

The Natural History Museum
Cromwell Road
London SW7 5BD

The top spot to visit here is the 'Human Biology Gallery', where you can learn things ranging from what it's like for a baby inside its mother's body to all the different jobs your blood does for you.

Body books

The Human Body Infographic Sticker Activity Book, Jo Dearden (Wayland, 2016)
Although it's aimed at quite young children, this book is a great fun way to discover all kinds of fascinating facts about the human body and its amazing abilities.

Utterly Amazing Human Body, Professor Robert Winston (DK Children, 2015)
Written by one of the world's top experts on how the human body develops, this book uses pull-outs, flaps and pop-ups to reveal some of the secrets of the human body.

The *Your Brilliant Body* series by Paul Mason (Wayland, 2015) gives you all the facts you need to know about how your body works, in a fun, easy-to-read way. It includes books on *Your Thumping Heart*, *Your Mind-Bending Brain*, *Your Growling Guts*, *Your Brilliant Bones*, *Your Breathtaking Lungs* and *Your Growing Body*.

Index

Cause Effect and Chaos!

Titles in this series:

In the Animal Kingdom

In Engineering and Industry

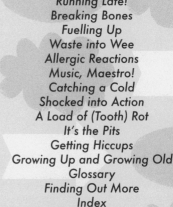
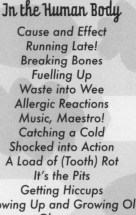

In the Human Body

In Outer Space

In the Rainforest

On Planet Earth